THE BIBLE STORY BEGINS

From Creation to Covenant

To J.Q. - a job well done

First published in the United States of America by Thomas Nelson, Inc., Publishers, Nashville, Tennessee, and distributed in Canada by Word Communications, Ltd., Richmond, British Columbia

Text by John Drane

The author asserts the moral right
to be identified as the author of this work

Published by
Lion Publishing plc
Sandy Lane West, Oxford, England
ISBN 0 7459 2171 X
Albatross Books Pty Ltd
PO Box 320, Sutherland, NSW 2232, Australia
ISBN 0 7324 0541 6

First edition 1994

Acknowledgments
Contributors to this volume
John Drane is Director of the Center for the Study of Christianity and Contemporary Society at the University of Stirling and the author of several highly acclaimed books on the Bible and its background. In this book he presents the Bible and its history in a way that young people can understand and enjoy.

Alan Millard, Rankin Professor of Hebrew and Ancient Semitic Languages at Liverpool University, is the consultant for the illustrations in this book, and all the books in this series.

Illustrators
All photos are copyright © Lion Publishing, except the following:
Ancient Art and Architecture Collection: 14 (middle left)
Ardea: 16 (frogs and midges)
British Museum: 5 (center)
M Necci: 7
Oxford Scientific Films: 2 (bottom left, bottom center), 16 (fish)
Zefa: 2 (top left, middle left, top center and extreme top left, middle center), 3, 5 (right), 12 (left)

The following Lion Publishing photographs appear by courtesy of:
the Trustees of the British Museum: 7 (top left, bottom left), 13 (left and center), 15 (left), 19
Haifa Maritime Museum: 12 (right)
Lepsius Denkmaler III: 11

Illustrations, copyright © Lion Publishing by:
Chris Molan: 1, 2, 3, 4 (right), 5 (top right), 6 (left), 7 (right), 8, 9, 10, 11 (bottom), 12, 13, 14, 15, 16 (bottom left), 17, 18 (top), 19, 20 (bottom)
Jeffrey Burn: 4 (left), 5 (bottom left), 6 (right), 7 (left), 11 (top), 16 (top), 18 (bottom), 20 (top)

Maps and graphics, copyright © Lion Publishing, by:
Oxford Illustrators Ltd: 7, 10, 12, 17

Bible quotations are taken from the Good News Bible, copyright ©American Bible Society, New York, 1966, 1971 and 4th edition 1976, published by the Bible Societies/HarperCollins, with permission.

Story text is based on material from *The Lion Children's Bible*, by Pat Alexander

ISBN 0-7852-7903-2

Printed and bound in Malaysia

12345-98979695

B·I·B·L·E WORLD

THE BIBLE STORY BEGINS

FROM CREATION TO COVENANT

John Drane

OLIVER NELSON

THOMAS NELSON PUBLISHERS

Nashville · Atlanta · London · Vancouver

Contents

page 1

page 8

page 9

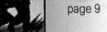

page 10

page 2

page 16

page 7

page 20

page 7

page 15

page 20

1 Why in the World?

► Where did the world come from?

► What's the point of being alive?

► Why is there so much wrongdoing in the world?

► Why is it sometimes hard to make decisions?

► Why is it often easier to do something wrong than to do something good?

► Why do bad things happen to good people?

► Why do people love to fight one another?

Life sometimes seems to be full of questions such as these—and short on answers.

The people who wrote the Bible knew how important these questions, and others like them, can be, so that is where they begin. But they also knew how hard it can be to understand the answers to questions like these. That is why they start with some stories. Telling stories is a good way to look into hard questions.

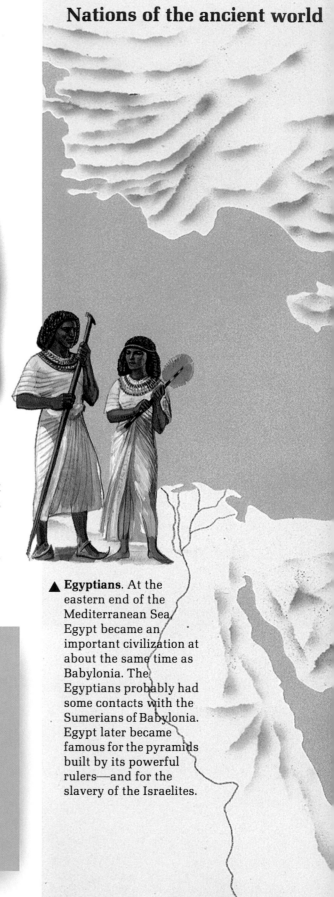

Big questions

The first stories in the Bible all deal with the big questions of life. Adam and Eve, Cain and Abel, and Noah are just some of the characters who appear in the stories. It is impossible to put a date on these people because the stories go right back to the beginning of time itself. They ask questions that people in all countries and at all times will always want to know about.

▲ **Egyptians.** At the eastern end of the Mediterranean Sea, Egypt became an important civilization at about the same time as Babylonia. The Egyptians probably had some contacts with the Sumerians of Babylonia. Egypt later became famous for the pyramids built by its powerful rulers—and for the slavery of the Israelites.

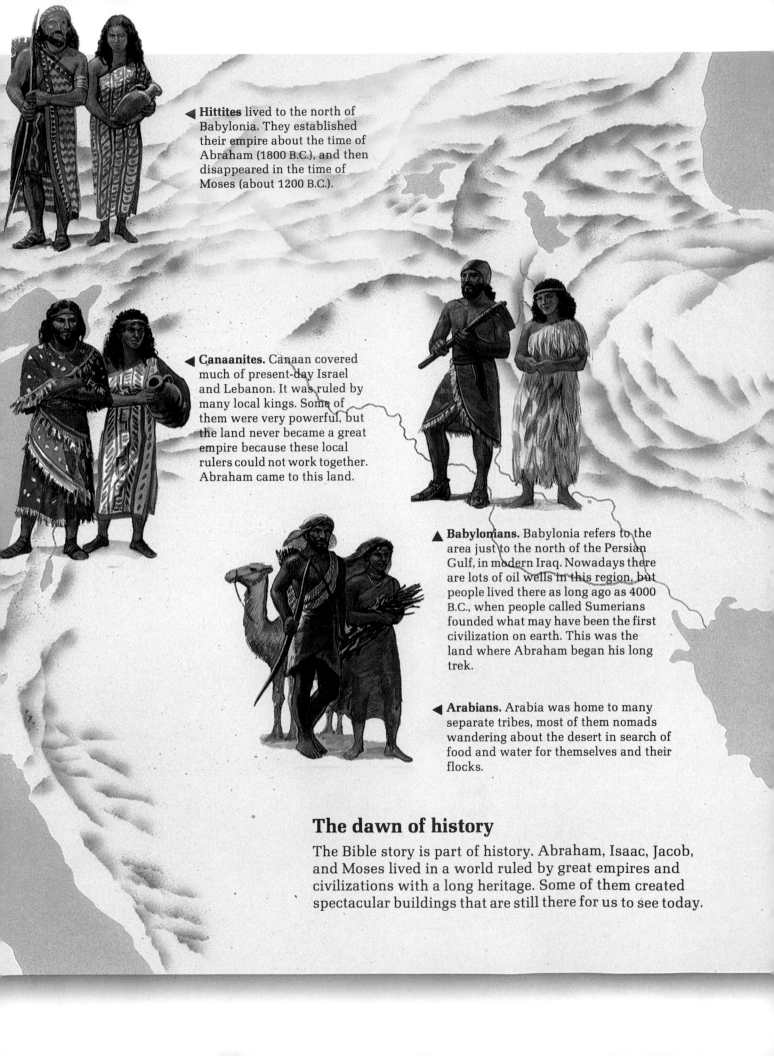

Hittites lived to the north of Babylonia. They established their empire about the time of Abraham (1800 B.C.), and then disappeared in the time of Moses (about 1200 B.C.).

Canaanites. Canaan covered much of present-day Israel and Lebanon. It was ruled by many local kings. Some of them were very powerful, but the land never became a great empire because these local rulers could not work together. Abraham came to this land.

Babylonians. Babylonia refers to the area just to the north of the Persian Gulf, in modern Iraq. Nowadays there are lots of oil wells in this region, but people lived there as long ago as 4000 B.C., when people called Sumerians founded what may have been the first civilization on earth. This was the land where Abraham began his long trek.

Arabians. Arabia was home to many separate tribes, most of them nomads wandering about the desert in search of food and water for themselves and their flocks.

The dawn of history

The Bible story is part of history. Abraham, Isaac, Jacob, and Moses lived in a world ruled by great empires and civilizations with a long heritage. Some of them created spectacular buildings that are still there for us to see today.

2 The Beginning of the World

The very first words of the Bible take the reader back to the start of all things:

"In the beginning God created the heavens and the earth."

Before anything else existed, God was always there.

Making the world

People of many nations have looked at the wonderful things in the world, and asked where it all came from. Of course, no one was actually around at the very beginning, so people all over the world have stories that try to explain it. The Bible begins with the creation story that was told in ancient Israel.

In the Bible book of Genesis (*genesis* means "beginning"), the story has seven sections, just like the seven days that make up a week. God does something different on each day. At the end of every day there is a kind of chorus saying, "God saw that it was good."

Day 1

began in darkness. All the life-forms on earth depend on light. So light was the very first thing God made.

Day 4

was when the sun and moon appeared.

Day 2

started with everything in chaos and covered with water. On this day, God made the sky.

Day 5

saw the birth of all kinds of birds and fish.

Day 3

dry land appeared, together with all kinds of plants.

Day 6

was when animals came into being, and eventually people.

God, people, and the environment

The world must have been very beautiful when everything was brand-new—quite different from the polluted earth we have now. Today, even good people are sometimes careless about looking after the environment. But the Bible has a special message:

God cares for all the animals and plants, and is concerned for their well-being.

People were made last, and depend on plants and animals for their survival.

People—women, men and children together—are given a special role to care for the rest of creation, and in this way to share in God's work.

Day 7

was God's day for rest—and for admiring this fantastic world.

The why and the how

For thousands of years, people thought the earth was like a flat disc, built on pillars coming up from the underworld, with the sky like a solid dome overhead. Science today gives quite a different view of things. But the Bible stories never tried to be scientific. They do not describe what the world is made of and how it came together as it did. They explain why the world exists and how people should live in it.

3 The Big Mistake

At the very beginning everything was calm and peaceful. Women and men lived in harmony—with the environment and with one another. But life is no longer like that. What can possibly have gone wrong?

Trusting God

Once, the Bible says, there were two people—Adam and Eve. They were husband and wife. Adam and Eve lived in a wonderful place—"the Garden of Eden"—where the natural world provided all they needed, and they in turn took good care of it. They treated each other as equal partners in all they did. Above all, they were friends with God. They knew they could trust God, and they did.

In return, God asked just one thing. The garden contained one very special tree, and God told them not to eat the fruit from it.

THE SPECIAL TREE

One day, as Eve was walking past the special tree, she heard the soft, hissing voice of a serpent. "See how good this fruit is. Doesn't it make your mouth water? Why not try it? The fruit will make you wise. If you eat it, you will be as smart as God!"

Eve looked at the fruit. She wanted to be as smart as God. She wanted to do as she liked. She stretched out her hand and picked it. Eve ate the forbidden fruit—and Adam did, too.

◀ **A lovely world**
The Bible story says that the world as God made it was very, very good.

Tragedy

Things always start to go wrong when people disobey God. The instant Adam and Eve ate the fruit, they knew it was wrong. Their lovely life was never the same again. They became suspicious of each other. They were ashamed to speak to God. Very soon, they left the beautiful garden for good. By disobeying God, they changed things forever. But worse was to come.

▲ **A cruel place**
The Bible says that when people turned away from God, the whole world was affected and became a cruel place.

Did you know?
The name *Adam* means "humankind." The Bible says that all the evil things that are in the world begin when ordinary people forget God's standards and live selfishly.

THE JEALOUS BROTHER

Adam and Eve had two sons, Cain and Abel. Cain became a farmer, Abel a shepherd. At harvest, Cain gave some of his crops as a thank-you present to God. Abel gave God one of his lambs. Cain became jealous and angry. He thought that God liked his brother's gift more than his own. Out in the fields one day, Cain killed Abel. He thought no one had seen him. But God knew.

4 Wrongdoing – and Punishment

The first stories in the Bible describe how the world went from bad to worse. After Cain murdered his brother Abel, violence increased everywhere. A man called Lamech boasted that when another person hurt him, he killed him in revenge.

Violence and evil

Within a very short time, law and order broke down completely. There was no justice or fair treatment for anyone. The world was so spoiled that, reluctantly, God could allow it no longer. Those who were behaving so badly must be punished for their deeds. Yet God still had a deep love for the world and its people and animals.

▼ **A floating box**
Although the Bible says quite a lot about the ark, it is still not clear what it would have looked like. However, it was intended to be a giant container that would float, not a ship that could go on a voyage—for during the flood, there was nowhere to go!

▲ **Big boats, little boats**
The ark that Noah built on dry land would have seemed vast—especially when compared to the little river boats that were used in ancient Babylonia. These were simply made from woven willow branches and covered with pitch or animal skins to make them waterproof.

THE GREAT FLOOD

Noah was a good man who lived as God's friend. But the world was full of evil. One day, God told Noah there had to be a fresh start. Everything would be swept away in a great flood.

"Build a boat," God said, "big enough for all your family, and two of every kind of animal and bird." Noah trusted God and began work.

People thought Noah was crazy building a boat on dry land. He told them what God said about the flood and invited them to join him. No one listened. But Noah worked on until the boat was finished.

When the boat was completed, Noah and his family and the birds and animals went inside it.

And then the rain came, just as God had said. It rained till there was water everywhere.

Only the people and animals in the boat were safe. At last the rain stopped. The water level fell slowly and Noah's boat came to rest on a hilltop. Noah wondered if the earth was dry enough for him to leave the boat. He opened a window and let out a raven. Then he let out a dove. But it was not yet dry enough, and the dove flew back to the boat.

Soon after, the dove flew out again and brought back a fresh green leaf from an olive tree. The third time, the dove flew off for good. The land was dry again.

Did you know?

A dove and an olive branch are often used as symbols of peace today. The idea comes from the story of the great flood: when Noah saw the dove with an olive twig, he knew that everything was going to be all right again.

5 After the Flood

According to the Bible, the great flood lasted for a long time. Rain fell for forty days, and the water kept on rising for five months. It was almost eight months before Noah's boat came to rest on a mountain—and two more months before anyone could see the mountain tops. By the time Noah and the animals left the boat, more than a year had gone by.

Absolutely every living creature and person not in the boat was destroyed. The only survivors were the people and the animals with Noah.

After the floodwaters went down, God made a solemn promise to Noah that such a great catastrophe would never ever happen again.

Other flood stories

The Bible is not the only ancient book to tell of a great flood. Fascinating stories of an ancient flood survive in many parts of the world. Some of the nations near to Israel told stories about a great flood that destroyed much of the world.

The story of Atrahasis was written by the Sumerians. It tells how the gods decided to destroy people when they discovered it was impossible to control them.

The *Epic of Gilgamesh* comes from Babylon. Its hero, Enlil, survived a great flood by building a large boat.

All these stories may have been related to one another at the very start. But there are some interesting differences:

In the Gilgamesh story, there are many gods who sent the flood because the people woke them up with all their chattering! The Bible story speaks of just one true God who sent the flood because of the disobedience and lawlessness of the people.

In other stories, the gods and goddesses do what they like. People are afraid of them because no one knows what they will think of next. The God of the Bible loves people and wants only what is best for them.

Did you know?

The boat in which Noah survived the great flood was about 436 feet long by 72 feet wide, and 43 feet high. Think about how big that is—each rectangle in the scale below is about the length of a modern bus.

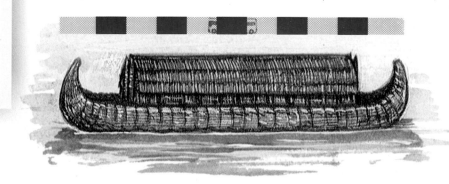

THE GREAT PROMISE

After the waters of the great flood had completely gone, Noah and his family built an altar and praised God. They cooked food and feasted—and worshiped and prayed—to thank God they were safe.

As they did so, the sun broke through and a beautiful rainbow arched right across the sky.

"See that rainbow," said God. "I've put it there for a special purpose. I'm making a promise to you, and to everyone who lives after you. Whenever you see the rainbow in the future, remember that this earth will never again be covered by such a terrible flood."

▲ Stories on clay tablets
A fragment of an ancient flood story, written thousands of years ago.

◄ The ark comes to ground
This is Mount Ararat in present-day Turkey. The Bible says that the ark grounded on a mountain in the Ararat range.

Did you know?
Nowadays, the rainbow is used as a sign of hope and healing for the environment. Today the world is threatened by pollution that people have made. The flood story says that God still cares for humanity and the well-being of the planet. But it also shows that there is punishment for those who do not respect God's plans.

6 A Tower to Heaven

The Bible stories show that, time and again, people have done wicked things. Even though God sent a great flood to destroy all their wickedness, they still did not learn. The story of their attempt to build a tower to heaven tells of one more mistake.

THE TALLEST TOWER IN THE WORLD

In the plains of Babylonia, people learned how to make bricks and use tar to hold them together. One day someone said, "Let's build ourselves a city, with a great tower, the tallest that has ever been built. That will make us really famous." Soon they were all hard at work, building a tower that would show how clever they were. It was called the Tower of Babel.

God watched them as the walls grew higher and higher, and the people got bigger and bigger ideas. God knew this would lead to trouble. These people believed they could do absolutely anything. They were beginning to think they were gods themselves!

God did not wait until the tower was finished before taking action. If people spoke different languages they would no longer understand one another. It would be more difficult to plot and plan together. So God mixed up their languages and scattered them to different parts of the world.

▶ **Carrying heavy loads**
The great buildings of ancient Babylonia were built using slave labor. Slaves may have carried loads of bricks on simple slings bound around their foreheads. This type of carrier was used until recent times.

Ancient stories and what they mean

The story of the Tower of Babel is the last of the ancient stories at the beginning of the Bible: creation, Adam and Eve, Noah, and the great flood. These stories give answers to the kind of questions that people in all times and places are always asking.

Some of the questions are about simple, everyday things:

▶ Where does the rainbow come from, and what does it mean?

It is a reminder of God's love, and the promise made to Noah that God would never again send a flood to destroy the world.

▶ Why are there so many languages in the world?

To remind people that when they try to be all-wise and all-powerful, they create only confusion.

Other questions are about the way people live:

▶ Why is life such a struggle?

▶ Why are farmers' crops attacked by so many pests and diseases?

▶ Why is there so much violence and hatred?

▶ Why do people injure and abuse even their own families?

People cannot live in peace with their environment and with other people because, like Adam and Eve, they disregard God's rules for living.

▶ Why do bad people often seem to get away with wrongdoing?

Because, in spite of their evil, God still loves them. But they won't get away with it forever. In the end, God will have to judge wrongdoing, just as He did with the great flood.

Ziggurats

Tall stepped towers called ziggurats were built in many Babylonian cities. Some were as large as the pyramids in Egypt. There is nothing wrong with magnificent buildings. But the Bible warns that human achievements can easily turn people aside from trusting in God.

7 God Makes a Promise

Abraham lived in the great city of Ur, just north of the Persian Gulf. When he received a message from God, his life changed. What followed has had a dramatic effect on the whole of world history ever since.

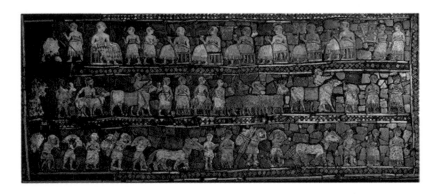

▲ **Treasures from Ur**
This mosaic picture is one of many treasures found in the royal graves of ancient Ur. These treasures show the skill of craftworkers several hundred years before Abraham's time.

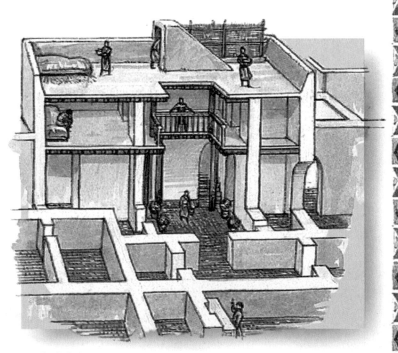

▲ **A rich home**
Archaeologists have discovered the remains of houses at Ur dating to the time of Abraham. The one in this diagram must have belonged to wealthy people; it had two floors, with rooms built around a courtyard. The room at the front was a chapel. The gold dish, like the mosaic above, is one of the treasures found at Ur.

A new land

Most people in the ancient world never traveled beyond their own village for the whole of their lives. Abraham and Sarah certainly never imagined they would leave their own country. It was a long journey to get to Canaan, traveling on donkeys for hundreds of miles to a strange land.

Canaan was an unsettled place to live. Babylon and Egypt were the two great superpowers of the day. They were great rivals, and fought many wars. Their armies often marched through Canaan, and many fierce battles were fought in this land.

These wars left lots of people homeless, and Abraham was not the only one who was on the move. Thousands of displaced people were searching for new places to live, where

ABRAHAM LEAVES TOWN

 In the city of Ur, in the country of Chaldea, there lived a man called Abraham. His wife's name was Sarah. One day God said to Abraham:

"I want you to leave Ur and go far away to the land of Canaan. There you will become the founder of a great nation."

Now Abraham and Sarah had no children. But they believed God and trusted this promise. Together with Lot, Abraham's nephew, and their servants, their flocks and herds, they left Ur. They left their home, and all their friends and relatives, and set out for an unknown land.

they would be safe from armies and could care for their flocks and bring up their children in peace.

Others were moving about because their fields had been ravaged by disease, and the poor harvests had led to famine.

Then there were nomads who just enjoyed a lifestyle in which they were continually on the move, traveling through the desert from one oasis to another, and occasionally spending short periods camped outside the cities where they could trade their goods.

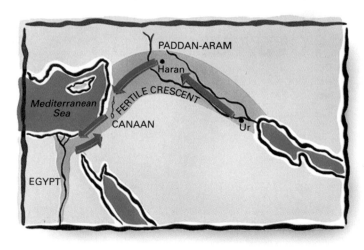

▲ The fertile crescent
In the ancient world, much of the Middle East was desert—as it still is today. So most people lived where it was not too hard to grow crops and feed herds of sheep and goats. Stretching from Babylon in the east to Egypt in the west was a great crescent-shaped area of good fertile land. It became known as the *fertile crescent*. Abraham moved from the eastern end of this crescent to the opposite end, not far from Egypt.

8 Abraham and His Family

God made a promise to Abraham: "I want to give a blessing to every family in the whole world, and I have chosen your family as the people to start with."

Abraham in Egypt

Abraham was rather puzzled by God's promise about his family. At the time, he had no children. When his wife, Sarah, was unable to have children, Abraham lost patience with God.

There was famine in Canaan, so Abraham and Sarah went to Egypt to find food. He was afraid the Egyptians would see how beautiful Sarah was and kill him so they could have her. So he said that she was his sister and not his wife. The plan worked. The king of Egypt wanted Sarah to be *his* wife. Abraham handed her over, and was given rich presents of flocks and servants in return. Sarah must have felt betrayed. But it made no difference. It was only after the king discovered Abraham's lies that Abraham was forced to admit his dishonesty.

Family problems

When Sarah still had no child, it became harder and harder to see how God's promise could come true. Abraham had already shown what a coward he was, putting Sarah at risk to save his own life. Sarah came up with a plan to give him what he wanted. Following the custom of the time, she gave him her Egyptian maid, Hagar, to have his child. In this way Abraham got a son, and called him Ishmael.

Later, Sarah did get pregnant, and had her own son, Isaac. Sarah was desperate that Isaac should inherit the family wealth, and wanted Abraham to send Hagar and Ishmael away.

This worried Abraham but he knew that God's promise about his family really meant Isaac. So he sent Hagar and Ishmael away.

Fortunately for them, God stepped in, and promised to Hagar that her son would also be the leader of a great nation.

Abraham and God

Abraham had made one mistake after another in trying to solve his problems. Did he have any trust left in God's promise?

The test came when Abraham was convinced God was telling him to kill his son Isaac. (In those days worship often included killing valuable animals as a sign of obedience to God.) If he went through with it, he would really have to rely on God to make the promise about his family come true. Abraham told neither his servants nor Isaac what he planned to do. He took Isaac off to a mountain, tied the boy tightly with ropes, and was about to kill him with a knife. Only when God stepped in at the very last moment was Isaac's life spared.

Trusting God

Abraham was certainly not a model husband or father. Sarah, Hagar, Ishmael, and Isaac—he betrayed them all at one time or another. Yet he truly wanted to love and serve God. Unlike the people of Noah's time, he knew when he'd made mistakes.

But God's promise could be trusted. God helped him pick up the pieces of his broken home and family life and in the end he became known as the man who trusted God.

▲ Nomads
The lifestyle of desert nomads has changed little from Abraham's day to the present.

9 The Twin Brothers

Isaac grew up, married, and had his own family. But his own unhappy childhood had left its mark on him, and he repeated some of the same mistakes his father Abraham had made. Yet in spite of his failures, God was still with him. The history of Isaac and his sons shows God's special concern for families.

Isaac marries

When the time came for Isaac to be married, his father, Abraham, was determined that he would not marry a Canaanite woman. Instead, Isaac's wife would come from the same race and culture as Abraham himself—back in Babylonia. All marriages at that time were arranged by parents, and Isaac would have expected his father to find him a wife.

The woman who was chosen was called Rebekah. Just as Abraham and Sarah had done, she had to leave her homeland and travel to the foreign country of Canaan.

Like Sarah, Rebekah was at first unable to have children. But she did become pregnant, and gave birth to twins. Both were boys, and they were born immediately after each other. In fact, the second to be born came so close behind his brother that his hand was grabbing the first one's heel! They were given the names Esau and Jacob.

Names

In the ancient world (and still in some places today) people's names were meant to say something about them.

Esau comes from a Hebrew word that means "red" or "reddish-brown," though it also sounds like another word that means "hairy." The story says he was both red and hairy.

Jacob means "someone who grabs by the heel," or "a person who cheats." He certainly lived up to this name later in life.

Esau's name described his appearance; Jacob's name described the kind of person he was to become. He was always trying to get the best for himself. When his father was old and likely to die, he went ahead with a really selfish trick to cheat Esau out of what was his.

▲ Rich gifts
Abraham's steward brought rich gifts for Isaac's bride, including a nose ring and bracelets. This gold jewelry discovered in an ancient tomb of that time shows what they may have looked like.

JACOB'S SELFISH TRICK

When Isaac was old he began to go blind. In those days, it was the custom for a father, before he died, to ask God's special blessing on the eldest son. Isaac decided it was time to give Esau his blessing. But first he sent Esau out to hunt for meat to make a good stew.

Rebekah overheard what Isaac said to Esau, and she made up her mind that Jacob, who was her favorite, should have the blessing. Isaac was almost blind. Jacob could pretend to be Esau, and Isaac would never know.

So, while Esau was still out hunting, Rebekah made one of her tastiest, spiciest stews from the meat of two young goats. And she spread the goatskins over Jacob's smooth arms and neck to make them feel like Esau's rough, hairy skin.

Jacob dressed up in his brother's clothes, and took the meal in to his father. The lovely smell from the food, and the feel of the skins, deceived Isaac. But he thought the voice sounded different.

"Are you really Esau?" he asked.

"I am," Jacob lied.

So Isaac gave Jacob the special blessing the first son always received.

Jacob the deceiver

Jacob succeeded in his plan to steal the blessing that really was Esau's. This was a very serious thing. Once the blessing had been given, no one could take it back—not even Isaac. And whoever had the blessing would inherit all his father's wealth and possessions. It is no wonder that Esau was very angry—Jacob had deceived even his own father. Jacob was forced to leave home.

Jacob's Story

Jacob suffered for the selfish way he tricked his brother. He had to run away to make a new life for himself. Things did not always go well for him, and he learned some important lessons.

A special promise

Isaac had given the blessing to Jacob, and the promises God made to his grandfather Abraham now belonged to him. One night, Jacob was sleeping in the open air, using a stone for his pillow, when he had a dream. Angels were going up and down on a ladder. As Jacob watched, he heard a voice. It was God.

"I am with you," God said. "I will look after you wherever you go, and take you safely back to your own land."

After all the trouble he had caused, Jacob must have been relieved.

The trickster tricked

Jacob settled in the household of his uncle Laban. Laban seemed kind and generous, but he was really just like Jacob—crafty and selfish. Jacob fell in love with Rachel, one of Laban's daughters. Laban agreed they could marry, but then played a nasty trick. On the wedding day, Jacob was forced to marry Rachel's sister Leah instead. He had already worked for seven years without wages to be allowed to marry Rachel. Laban agreed that he could marry Rachel one week later. But in return, he demanded that Jacob work for him for another seven years.

Jacob and Esau

Jacob knew it was wrong not to make peace with his brother Esau. When his years of working for Laban were up, he left Laban's home and made his way back to see Esau. Jacob was nervous about what would happen when they met. He need not have worried: Esau had done well for himself, and welcomed his brother with open arms. But on the way Jacob himself had changed. The turning point was a fight with a stranger.

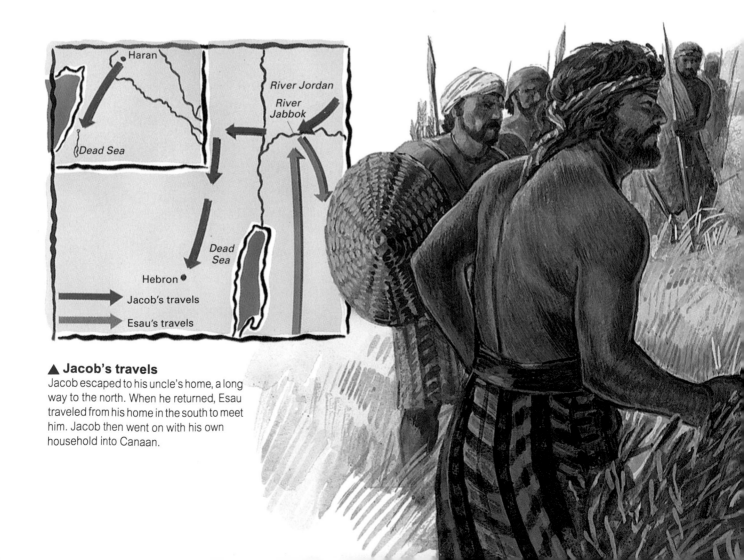

▲ **Jacob's travels**
Jacob escaped to his uncle's home, a long way to the north. When he returned, Esau traveled from his home in the south to meet him. Jacob then went on with his own household into Canaan.

THE STRANGE FIGHT

After long years away, Jacob set off for home. One night on the journey, he lay down to sleep by the River Jabbok. A Man came and wrestled with him all night until dawn. Jacob did not recognize Him, but he knew He came from God, and he refused to let the Man go until He had given him God's blessing.

The stranger was stronger than Jacob and, as they wrestled, Jacob's leg was injured. From then on he always walked with a limp.

The fight changed Jacob in other ways too, and so he was given a new name. He was no longer called "Jacob," the man who cheats, but "Israel," the man who has come face to face with God.

Jacob, Israel, and God

Like Abraham and Isaac before him, Jacob was delighted when God promised a great future for his family. Like them, though, he thought his own ideas were better than God's. As he wrestled with the stranger by the river, he even believed he was stronger than God. But when his leg was injured, he learned his lesson.

From that day on, Jacob knew he was not as powerful as he thought he was. His new name, Israel, became the name of the nation who descended from him. As the years passed, the Israelites too found it difficult to trust God, and they often made the same kinds of mistakes as Abraham, Isaac, and Israel. But God never gave up on them.

Joseph the Dreamer

Great changes lay ahead for the family of Jacob, now called Israel. At the center of events was one of Jacob's sons, Joseph.

There were eleven other sons, and a daughter, from four different mothers. It was hardly surprising that they did not all get along with one another. In time, Jacob's own children began to quarrel in the same way that he had quarrelled with his brother and other relatives.

Jacob and his children

People learn how to be parents to their children by copying what happened to them in their own childhood. None of Jacob's ancestors had a happy family life. His grandfather Abraham and his father, Isaac—as well as his mother, Rebekah—had made serious mistakes. Jacob was just the same. Despite all that had happened to him, he found it hard to change and live differently. Instead of treating all his children equally, he had just one special favorite: Joseph, who was a son of his favorite wife, Rachel.

Did you know?
Jacob had twelve sons: Reuben, Simeon, Levi, Judah, Issachar and Zebulun (sons of Leah); Joseph and Benjamin (Rachel's sons); Dan and Naphtali (sons of Bilhah, Rachel's servant girl); and Gad and Asher (sons of Zilpah, Leah's servant girl).

The Bible also says that Jacob had a daughter named Dinah. She was Leah's child.

▲ **A coat of many colors**
An ancient tomb painting shows people wearing multi-colored coats. Joseph's special coat may have been like this.

THE FAVORITE

Jacob spoiled his favorite son, Joseph. He dressed him in a beautiful coat. It was the kind of coat worn only by princes. His brothers looked at the coat. They knew it meant special favors for Joseph.

This made all the brothers jealous. They had worked hard for their father. It was incredibly unfair for Joseph to have so much more than they did.

But there was worse to come. Joseph began to have dreams—and in his dreams the whole of his family were bowing down to him. When Joseph boasted about this, his brothers couldn't stand it any longer.

One day, Joseph left home to visit his brothers, who were away looking after the flocks. The brothers saw their chance.

"Let's kill him," they said. "We can tell our father he was attacked by wild animals."

Only Reuben refused to join in. He got them to throw Joseph down a dry well instead of killing him.

But when Reuben was not there, some merchants came by with laden camels, taking precious goods to sell in the markets of the big cities. Judah saw another opportunity for revenge.

"Come on," he said. "We can sell Joseph as a slave."

They pulled Joseph out of the well, and struck a deal with the traders. They kept Joseph's coat, stained it with blood, and then set off to show it to Jacob. He wept when he saw it. Some wild animal must have killed his son.

▶**Slave traders**
Many traders passed through Canaan, because it had several good routes between the wealthy empires of Babylonia and Egypt. In the ancient world, people were often sold as slaves. Joseph was taken across the hot desert to be sold in the markets of Egypt.

Did you know?
People in ancient times took dreams very seriously indeed. In both Babylon and Egypt, "dream books" were put together, and people consulted them for advice. Kings would always consult wise teachers to find out what their dreams meant. They thought of dreams as special messages from the gods—and believed they would come true in real life. No wonder Joseph's brothers hated him when he announced that, in his dreams, they were all serving him!

The Egyptians

Egypt was one of the two great empires of the time of Joseph. Its rulers actually controlled the land of Canaan, where Joseph came from.

Egypt's history can be traced back to at least 3000 B.C. Right from the very beginning, Egypt was ruled by kings known as pharaohs. The culture of ancient Egypt was very old by the time the Israelite nation began, and it continued long after, until the Romans conquered the land. In that time, there were thirty different dynasties, or royal families.

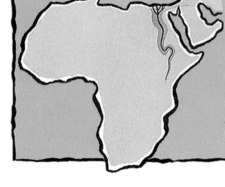

▲ A fertile valley
The area shaded green on this map shows the rich farmlands created by the annual flooding of the Nile.

▼ Eternal triangles
Many of the ancient buildings still standing in Egypt are connected with death. The pyramids are tombs where pharaohs and other important people were buried. The Egyptians were certain that there was another life after death. They carefully embalmed dead bodies and buried them with all kinds of treasures alongside them, for use in the next life.

A rich land

The River Nile runs through Egypt and in ancient times it flooded every year, leaving behind a layer of fertile soil. The crops that could be grown made Egypt a very rich land. Egyptian flax was renowned throughout the world, and the linen cloth made from flax fibers was in great demand.

Egyptian farmers could grow many different vegetables and fruits, too, as well as raising cattle, geese and ducks for food.

The only thing Egypt did not have was strong wood for houses and ships. But this could be imported quite easily from Phoenicia.

There was no shortage of natural stone, which was used to construct magnificent buildings in the desert sands. Many of these can still be seen today, unlike ancient buildings made of bricks, which crumbled away centuries ago.

▶Many gods

Religious beliefs in Egypt changed over the centuries. But for most of ancient history, the Egyptians thought of the pharaoh himself as a god. They believed in many other gods and goddesses as well.

Some were associated with places—such as Ptah, the god of Memphis, Khnum, god of the first bends in the Nile, and the crocodile god Sobek, who was god of the Faiyum area.

There was also Nut, goddess of heaven, Geb, god of the earth, and Ra, god of the sun. Others looked after different aspects of life—such as Maat, goddess of truth and justice, and Sekhmet, goddess of war.

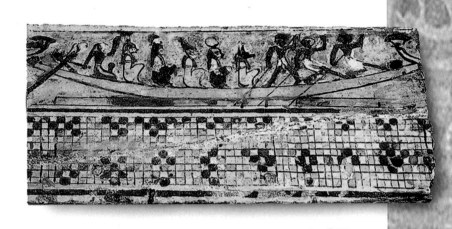

M   I   E   C   N

Hieroglyphs

The ancient Egyptians used picture symbols called hieroglyphs for writing. The simpler versions could be drawn in pen and ink.

13 Joseph to the Rescue

Joseph must have felt his dreams were shattered when his brothers sold him to slave traders. But in Egypt, he became rich and famous— and very powerful.

▼ **A sign of rank**
When the Egyptian pharaoh promoted Joseph to an important job, he gave him his second chariot as a sign of his rank.

Joseph's rise to fame

When Joseph first reached Egypt he became the slave of a rich woman, the wife of a top Egyptian official called Potiphar.

Potiphar's wife gave Joseph a hard time, and he ended up in prison.

Pharaoh's butler and baker were put in the same jail. They had dreams, and Joseph told them what they meant.

Pharaoh himself had a dream: seven weak cows ate up seven healthy cows. No one knew what it meant, but the pharaoh's butler, who was by then out of prison, suggested he ask Joseph.

"After seven years of really good harvests, there will be seven years of famine," Joseph said. "If you are wise, you will start to plan for it now."

The pharaoh was impressed and made Joseph his chief assistant, with the job of storing food ready for when the famine would come.

THE TERRIBLE FAMINE

Times were hard in Canaan: the harvest had failed, and there was no pasture for the flocks. Joseph's father, Jacob, and his brothers were still alive, but they were desperately hungry.

Jacob heard that the Egyptians had stores of food.

"You must go and ask if they will sell us any," he said.

The brothers packed up and set off on the journey. The youngest, Benjamin, stayed at home. He was the only one who had the same mother as Joseph, and Jacob wanted to take extra care of him.

The brothers were brought before a top Egyptian official. It was Joseph. They didn't know him, but he recognized them. When he saw that Benjamin was missing, he insisted they must come again bringing their other brother with them. But Joseph didn't tell them who he really was.

▲ **Corn harvest**
Scribes record the corn harvest in ancient Egypt.

When Benjamin arrived, Joseph could hardly hold back his tears. But he was still wary of the brothers who had treated him so badly, and he decided to set them a test.

After a great feast, Joseph sent the brothers on their way laden with food. But he had secretly hidden a valuable cup in Benjamin's sack and he sent his servant after them. The cup was found, and they returned.

"The one in whose sack my cup was found shall be my slave," said Joseph. "The rest can go free." He wondered if they would leave Benjamin to his fate.

But they were horrified. "Let me be your slave instead," Judah said. Then Joseph knew his brothers really were sorry for the way they had treated him all those years before, and he told them who he was.

A happy ending

Joseph's story had a happy ending. Joseph was reunited with his father, Jacob, and the whole family settled in Egypt.

They never thought of it as their home. When Jacob died, his body was taken to Canaan to be buried. And before he died, Joseph made his family promise faithfully that they would take his bones with them when they went to their own land.

The family knew God's promise to Abraham was that Canaan was to be their home. Although they stayed in Egypt for many years, living peacefully alongside the Egyptian people, their future lay elsewhere.

Slaves in Egypt

Jacob's family and their descendants did well in Egypt. As the years went by and babies were born, there were more and more of them. Soon Jacob's descendants—the Israelites—were a nation.

A new pharaoh

Joseph had welcomed his family to stay in Egypt, but the welcome did not last forever. Years later, a new pharaoh came to power. He did not care too much for these foreigners who had settled in his country. He devised a cruel plan to keep them under control.

▼ **Splendors for the pharaoh**
The proud and ambitious pharaoh who made the Israelites work as slaves ordered the construction of many splendid buildings.

◀ **A brick made by Israelites?**
Archeologists have discovered this ancient brick, which had the name of the pharaoh Rameses II impressed on it when it was just a block of wet clay. Rameses was probably the pharaoh who ruled at the time the Israelites left Egypt.

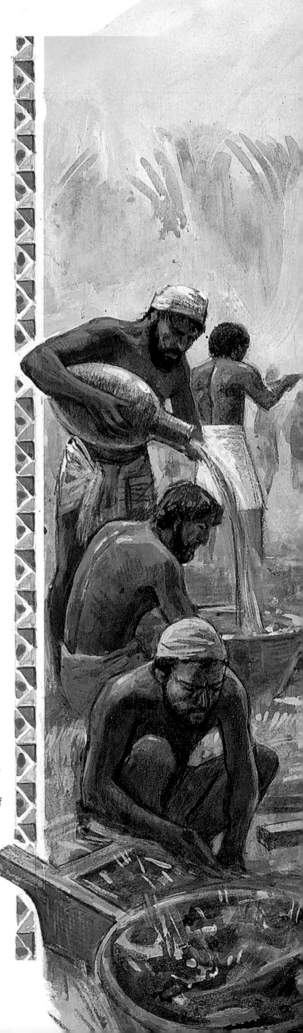

SLAVE LABOR

The Egyptian pharaoh was afraid: the Israelites who lived in his land were becoming a large group of people. One day they might turn against him. He must take control before it was too late.

He decided to make the Israelites his slaves. Cruel slave drivers forced them to work. The Israelites had to obey. Day after day, from morning to night, they toiled out in the sun, making bricks out of mud for Pharaoh. With these bricks, they were ordered to build two great cities, Pithom and Rameses.

The Israelites were very unhappy. At first, some of them thought of disobeying the slave drivers. But soon they were too weary to care. Life was just a miserable struggle from start to finish, and there seemed no way to change anything.

Egyptian royal families

The pharaoh who promoted Joseph belonged to a royal family called the Hyksos. They were not themselves true Egyptians, and that is probably why they found it easier to welcome people from a different nation.

But the Hyksos pharaohs lost power in 1570 B.C., and the pharaoh who made the Israelites slaves belonged to a different royal family. He was probably Rameses II, who ruled from 1290 to 1224 B.C. Rameses was a native-born Egyptian with a long Egyptian ancestry behind him.

15 Moses: the Adopted Prince

The Egyptian rulers tried everything to wipe out the Israelite people. They even told the midwives who delivered Israelite babies to kill any boys who were born. When the midwives disobeyed, one escaped this fate, and he was to hold the key to Israel's future.

▶An Egyptian princess
Moses was found and adopted by an Egyptian princess. He was brought up in great luxury, while his family continued to live as poor slaves.

THE BABY IN THE BASKET

An Israelite woman called Jochebed had a baby. She already had two children, a boy called Aaron and a girl called Miriam. When she saw the new baby was a boy she was terribly afraid. Pharaoh had ordered the death of every new baby boy in Israel. So she hid him for three months. But babies won't stay quiet and still for long. What was she to do?

Then she had an idea. She made a basket out of reeds and covered it with tar, to make it watertight. She put the baby inside. Then she took the basket and placed it among the tall reeds at the river's edge. She told Miriam to keep watch.

Very soon the king's daughter came down to the river to bathe, as Jochebed knew she would. When she saw the basket she sent her servant to fetch it. They opened the lid, and there inside was the loveliest baby they had ever seen. The princess knew this was an Israelite baby. But she had no children and decided to bring him up as her own son. She decided to call him Moses.

New hope

The people of Israel had a tremendous struggle for survival. Everything seemed to be against them. There was no way they could escape the cruelty and oppression of their Egyptian slave masters. But the birth of Moses was the start of a new episode in their history.

A baby and a mother, and midwives who disobeyed the pharaoh's orders—these may not seem like strong people who would overthrow a vicious tyrant. But their story was part of the promise that God had given.

Strong and confident characters like Abraham and Jacob had made a lot of problems for themselves because they were unwilling to trust God completely. Now it was the time for powerless people to see what God could do for them.

▲ The water's edge

Moses' family tried to keep their baby safe by hiding him in a floating basket among the papyrus that grew thickly by the water's edge. In ancient Egypt, people made coiled baskets from papyrus stems. A coating of pitch made Moses' basket waterproof.

16 Escape from Slavery

Moses faced a tough question as he grew up. Was he an Egyptian, like the mother who had adopted him, or an Israelite, as he knew he had been born?

One day he saw a slave master beating an Israelite slave so fiercely, he couldn't help attacking the man there and then. In fact, he killed him. When the story of this leaked out, he was forced to run away to save his own life. Out in the desert he became a shepherd.

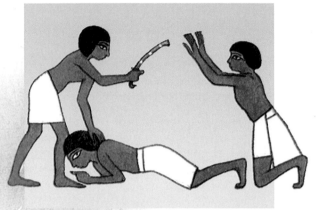

▲ **Slave drivers**
A slave receives a beating in ancient Egypt.

THE FLAMES IN THE BUSH

Moses was no longer a prince of Egypt. He was a shepherd spending long hours alone in the desert looking after his flocks. One day, he saw a very strange sight. A bush seemed to be on fire—but the fire didn't burn it up. Moses went to take a closer look.

"Stand back," said a voice, "and take off your shoes: this is holy ground."

Moses was afraid, but the voice went on:

"I am God: the God your ancestors knew and worshiped. I have seen the cruel sufferings of my people. You are to go to the king of Egypt, and get them set free. Bring them out of Egypt, into this desert, where they can worship me and learn what it means to trust me again."

Did you know?

When he met God at the burning bush, Moses asked, "What is your name, so I can tell Pharaoh who is sending me?" The answer was, "I am who I am."

In Hebrew, the letters of God's personal name are YHWH. The Jewish people never spoke this special name, and generally called God "the Lord." But the word may have been pronounced "Yahweh."

Moses meets Pharaoh

When Moses saw the flames in the bush and heard God speaking to him, he was terrified. After all, he was a wanted man in Egypt, because he had killed an Egyptian. Even if he did manage to get to see Pharaoh, what could he possibly say?

But he did go, taking his brother Aaron with him to do the talking.

Pharaoh said he wasn't interested in Moses' God and the promise to Abraham's family. Though he knew that he was treating the Israelites unfairly, he certainly didn't want to let go of such cheap slave labor.

But God gave Moses special power to show that this request had to be taken seriously. Soon the land was hit by a whole series of plagues that made Pharaoh begin to change his mind.

The plagues

The plagues were a series of disasters that struck Egypt to prove to Pharaoh that the God of Moses was a power to be reckoned with.

- The River Nile turned as red as blood. It smelled awful, and many fish died.

- A week later the whole land was swarming with frogs.

- Next there were swarms of insects and flies. Cattle began to die—even healthy ones.

- A disease that caused painful boils spread through the land.

- Great hailstones came and flattened the crops, even killing cattle.

- Swarms of locusts ate up every plant in sight.

- Then there was pitch darkness for three days.

- Last and worst of all, the oldest son of every family died.

The Long Journey

As long as Pharaoh refused to let the Israelites go free, the plagues continued. Some of these disasters affected the Israelites as well as the Egyptians. But not the final one, when the oldest son in each family died. God told Moses what the Israelites must do so that death would pass over their homes.

The Passover night

The last and worst disaster was going to strike in the night. Following Moses' instructions, the Israelite slaves held a special meal in their homes. They ate roast lamb, herbs, and bread made quickly without yeast. But before they ate, they splashed some of the blood of the lamb over the doorposts of their homes. As a result, their sons were safe. Death really did "pass over" their homes, which is why their meal came to be called *Passover*. Jewish families today still eat a Passover meal once a year, and remember the way God saved their ancestors: not just from the plague of death but also from slavery itself, because it gave the Israelites the chance to escape from Egypt.

The great escape

The great escape of the Israelite slaves from Egypt is usually called the *exodus*. This is the name of the Bible book which tells the story. It means "the going out" or "escape."

A CHANCE TO ESCAPE

The Egyptians were in great distress. The firstborn son had died in every family. People were weeping and wailing.

Pharaoh knew why this terrible thing had happened. It was another sign of the power of the Israelites' God, who wanted Pharaoh to set the people free. Now Pharaoh couldn't wait to get rid of them. The Egyptian people actually gave them gold and silver jewelry and fine clothes to take with them.

The Israelites hurried as quickly as they could to the borders of Egypt. And a good thing, too—because Pharaoh changed his mind and called out the army.

By the time the Israelites reached the Red Sea, the Egyptian army was close behind. There was water in front of them, and soldiers behind them. The people were terrified.

But Moses stretched out his arm, and God sent an east wind. All night it blew, clearing a pathway through the water for the Israelites to cross in safety.

But when the Egyptians tried to follow, the water rushed back and they were drowned. So, through Moses, God saved the people and led them out of Egypt to freedom.

Free at last

Over the border, the Israelites found a very strange landscape. It was desert, with no water to drink and little food to eat. Some of them grumbled to Moses.

"We were better off in Egypt," they said. "At least we had food and homes there—even though we were slaves."

But Moses knew this was all part of God's plan. Centuries before, God had promised that Abraham's descendants would become a great nation living in the land of Canaan. And the people soon found that God was indeed caring for them even in the desert: there was water to drink and food to eat in the most unlikely places.

The long way around
The Israelites took a long route to Canaan to avoid meeting other enemies. At Kadesh Barnea they sent spies out, but the report on the land they had traveled to so discouraged them that they turned back—and then spent many years in the desert.

(Map labels: CANAAN, Mediterranean Sea, River Jordan, Dead Sea, Kadesh-barnea, GOSHEN, EGYPT, River Nile, SINAI, Mount Sinai)

Whose side is God on?

The story of the Israelites' escape has given hope to many people since. In the nineteenth century, African people who had been taken to America by force to work as slaves were inspired by the fact that God took sides not with the rich and powerful pharaoh, but with the poor, exploited slaves.

To this day, wherever there is injustice and suffering, the story is an encouragement to the weak. It tells them that God is on the side of right, and will give weak people the strength to break free from those who are hurting them, no matter how long it takes.

18 Desert Life

When Moses first asked Pharaoh to let the Israelites go, he said they wanted to worship God in the desert. The Bible story has a lot to say about how they did that.

▼ The Sinai desert
The dry and dusty Sinai desert is a harsh place to live. Yet here the Israelites learned more of God's concern for them.

Israel in the desert

Like all other desert dwellers, the escaping slaves lived as nomads. They traveled from one oasis to another, looking for food and water for themselves and grazing for their sheep and goats. They took tents made of animal skins with them.

They soon learned to adapt to the desert life. They joined up with other tribes who were distantly related to them, and it was not long before they were a much larger band than the group of slaves who had escaped from Egypt.

Moses always tried to encourage them all to trust in God, but it was a hard job for him. Those who had been slaves knew they could never have got free by their own efforts. They had given up all hope of ever having a land of their own to live in. They knew that all they had was given to them by God. But their relatives who had never lived in Egypt had not shared this experience, and they were more inclined to think they could solve their problems in their own way.

Moses never gave up listening to God, and told the people time and again God's instructions for how they should live and how they should worship.

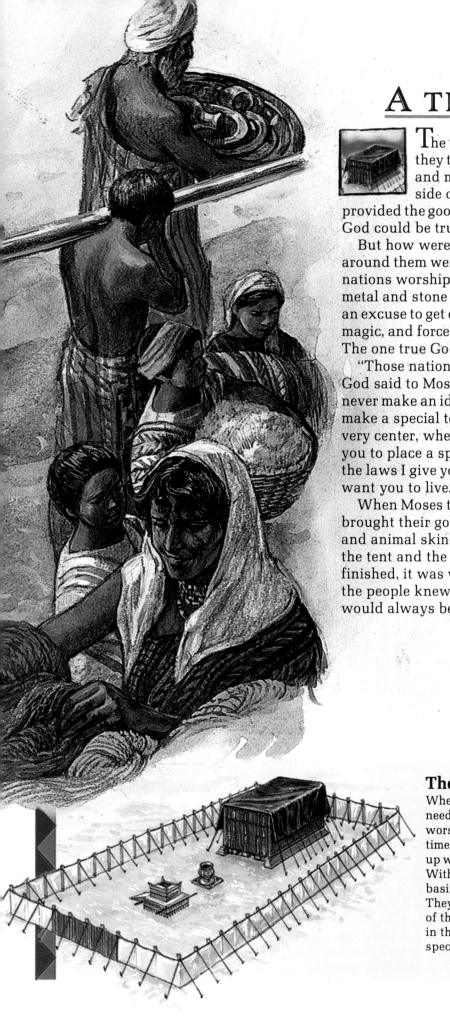

A TENT FOR GOD

The Israelites had escaped from Egypt. As they traveled in the desert, they learned more and more about God. Their God was on the side of the weak and the poor. Their God provided the good things they needed to stay alive. Their God could be trusted.

But how were they to worship God? The religions around them weren't a good example. Some of the other nations worshiped many gods, and they made idols of metal and stone to represent them. Their festivals were an excuse to get drunk for days at a time. They practiced magic, and forced people to do things against their will. The one true God hated all these things.

"Those nations disgust me with their evil practices," God said to Moses. "You will be different. You must never make an idol to represent me. But I do want you to make a special tent, where I can be worshiped. At the very center, where other people put their idols, I want you to place a special golden box. It will hold a copy of the laws I give you, so that no one will ever forget how I want you to live."

When Moses told them what God wanted, the people brought their gold and jewels, silver and bronze, linen and animal skins. Craftworkers set to work to make the tent and the things that went inside. When it was finished, it was very beautiful. A cloud covered it, and the people knew that God was truly pleased—and would always be with them.

The tent of meeting

When they lived in the desert, the people of Israel needed a portable tent where God could be worshiped because they were on the move all the time. The tent of meeting, or "tabernacle," was set up within an enclosure screened by linen hangings. Within the enclosure was also an altar and a huge basin containing water for ceremonial washing. They took great care of the tent and the golden ark of the covenant. Centuries later, when they settled in their own land, these became part of a spectacular temple in their capital city.

19 Laws for a Good Life

While they were in the desert, the people of Israel received the laws that told them how God wanted them to live. At the center of them were ten great laws that are still admired and kept by people all over the world today.

The Ten Commandments

One day, Moses went to the top of a great mountain to meet with God. The people watched from the bottom, and when they saw a thick cloud covering the mountain and heard thunder breaking over it, they knew something very special was taking place. God had ten special things to say to Moses and the people.

I am God, the one who rescued you from slavery in Egypt. Serve no other gods but me.

Never make idols, or bow down to them.

Treat my name with respect.

Keep my day of rest, the seventh day of each week.

Show respect to your parents.

Never murder another human being.

Husbands and wives: be loyal to each other.

You shall not steal.

You shall not tell lies.

Never be greedy for the things that other people have.

Did you know?

The ten great laws, or Ten Commandments, are all about relationships. They are arranged in two sections.

The first four are about the relationship between people and God. They say important things about the way the Israelites should think about and worship God. The laws are followed by Jews and Christians.

The other six are laws about the kind of relationships people should have with one another. Ever since they were given, these laws have formed the basis of civilized life in many parts of the world. People have not always been able to keep them, but many look up to them as the ideal way to live.

The first commandment reminded the Israelites that God had rescued them from slavery in Egypt. They must never forget that. They had all been equal at the beginning, because they had all been slaves, and had nothing. Other laws said that debts between people had to be canceled after seven years, so that no one would get rich at the expense of others. It was a hard lesson to learn but it was what God wanted.

Did you know?

Moses received the Ten Commandments on Mount Sinai. It is sometimes also called Mount Horeb in the Bible. There is more than one high mountain in the desert between Egypt and Canaan, but most people think Sinai was Jebel Musa, an imposing granite peak 7,362 feet high in the southern part of the Sinai peninsula.

Golden calf

Moses was away some time receiving the laws. Meanwhile, the people made an idol in the shape of a calf, like the ones in Egypt, and worshiped that! It may have looked rather like this model of a calf, also from ancient times.

The Agreement

The Israelites did not always find it easy to live as God wanted. But when Moses explained God's laws to them, they gladly and willingly agreed to live by them. Their acceptance of God's demands was at the heart of the agreement—the covenant—that God made with them.

Making a covenant

People in the ancient world made covenants—agreements—for all sorts of purposes. A covenant was a way of spelling out how people would deal with one another. The Hittites were a strong empire for five hundred years before the time of Moses, and when they conquered other nations they made covenants with them. Hittite covenants and God's covenant with Moses are set out in a similar way. These are some of the sections:

▶ **An introduction.** The Hittite king would name himself, just as God does in the Ten Commandments.

▶ **A historical reminder.** The Hittite king told the other nation all the good things he had done for their benefit. God reminded Israel how they were rescued from Egypt.

▶ **The laws.** Kings normally demanded that people fight in their armies. God's laws were about how people should live.

▶ **Safekeeping.** Such an important agreement had to be kept in a special place—a temple or palace, perhaps. God's laws were to be placed in the golden ark of the covenant and kept in the tent the Israelites made for God.

▶ **Witnesses were named.** Witnesses were people or objects who had seen and heard the solemn agreement being made. The Bible says Moses set up twelve stone pillars to be witnesses—one for each of Israel's twelve tribes, each descended from Jacob's sons.

▶ **Penalties.** The final section listed the penalties for those who broke the law, and the benefits for those who kept it. Moses gave the people a long list of each.

The covenant between God and Israel followed this pattern because it was a standard way of making an agreement at that time. But Israel's covenant didn't begin there. God had already made special promises to Noah, Abraham, Isaac, Jacob, and finally Moses. Experience showed that God could be trusted to keep these promises, and that made this agreement special.

Did you know?

The agreement between God and the Israelites is often called *covenant*. Another word for it is *testament*.

The Christian Bible has two main sections, the Old Testament and the New Testament.

▼ **The ark of the covenant**
The ark of the covenant box was carried on two poles. This chest, which belonged to an Egyptian king, was carried in the same way.

Laws and festivals

There are many more laws besides the Ten Commandments. As well as the laws in the book called Exodus, there are long lists of laws in three other books: Leviticus, Numbers, and Deuteronomy. Some of them are about the details of everyday life for the Israelites at that time. Many are about how to worship God, and they describe the religious festivals of Israel.

● **Passover.** This festival recalls the night the Israelites made their escape from Egypt.

● **Weeks, or Pentecost.** Fifty days after Passover was a time to celebrate the grain harvest.

● **Trumpets.** The seventh month of the year was the New Year festival.

● **Day of Atonement.** On this day the people asked God's forgiveness for all their wrongdoing. The priest made special offerings to God on this day in the tent Israel made for God.

● **Tabernacles.** At the time of the fruit harvest, the people camped out in shelters made of branches (*tabernacles*) to remember their ancestors' life as desert nomads.

A trumpet call

Priests blew a ram's horn (a *shofar*) to announce the beginning of a festival and to call the people together.

▼ Tabernacles

Celebrating the feast of tabernacles centuries after the Exodus.

Finding Out More

If you want to know more about what you've read in *The Bible Story Begins*, you can look up the stories in the Bible.

The usual shorthand method has been used to refer to Bible passages. Each Bible book is split into chapters and verses. Take **Exodus 20:1–17**, for example. This refers to the book of Exodus; chapter 20; verses 1–17.

1   Why in the World?

Genesis 2:7–3:24; Genesis 4:1–16; Genesis 6:5–9:17

Genesis 12:1–25:11; Genesis 21:1–35:29; Genesis 25:20–49:33; Exodus 2:1– Deuteronomy 34:8   **The dawn of history**

Genesis 11:27–31; Exodus 1:1–14; Genesis 12:5–7   **Nations of the ancient world**

2   The Beginning of the World

Genesis 1:1

Genesis 1:1–2:4   **Making the world**

3   The Big Mistake

Genesis 2; Genesis 3:1–6

Genesis 3:8–24   **Tragedy**

Genesis 4:1–16   **The jealous brother**

4   Wrongdoing—and Punishment

Genesis 4:19–24

Genesis 6:5–7   **Violence and evil**

Genesis 6:9–8:12   **The great flood**

5   After the Flood

Genesis 9:8–17

Genesis 6:15   **Did you know?**

Genesis 9:8–17   **The great promise**

6   A Tower to Heaven

Genesis 11:1–9   **The tallest tower in the world**

7   God Makes a Promise

Genesis 12:1–5   **Abraham leaves town**

8   Abraham and His Family

Genesis 12:10–20   **Abraham in Egypt**

Genesis 16:1–15   **Family problems**

Genesis 22:1–14   **Abraham and God**

9   The Twin Brothers

Genesis 26:7–11

Genesis 24:1–66; Genesis 25: 21–26   **Isaac marries**

Genesis 24:22   **Rich gifts**

Genesis 27:1–29   **Jacob's selfish trick**

Genesis 27:30–45   **Jacob the deceiver**

10   Jacob's Story

Genesis 28:10–15   **A special promise**

Genesis 29:1–30   **The trickster tricked**

Genesis 33:1–10   **Jacob and Esau**

Genesis 32:22–32   **The strange fight**

11   Joseph the Dreamer

Genesis 37:1–35   **The favorite**

13   Joseph to the Rescue

Genesis 39:1–41:57   **Joseph's rise to fame**

Genesis 42:1–45:8   **The terrible famine**

Genesis 41:42–43   **A sign of rank**

Genesis 46:1–47:12; Genesis 49:29–33; Genesis 50:24–26   **A happy ending**

Index